An Introduction to Coping with

Phobias

2nd Edition

An Introduction to Coping with
Phobias

2nd Edition

Brenda Hogan

ROBINSON

First published in Great Britain in 2007 by Robinson,
an imprint of Constable & Robinson Ltd

This edition published in 2017 by Robinson

1 3 5 7 9 10 8 6 4 2

Copyright © Brenda Hogan, 2007, 2017

A CIP catalogue record for this book
is available from the British Library.

Important note
This book is not intended as a substitute for medical advice
or treatment. Any person with a condition requiring medical
attention should consult a qualified medical practitioner
or suitable therapist.

ISBN: 978-1-47213-852-1

Typeset in Bembo by Initial Typesetting Services, Edinburgh
Printed and bound in Great Britain by CPI Group (UK) Ltd,
Croydon CR0 4YY

Papers used by Robinson are from well-managed forests
and other responsible sources.

Robinson
An imprint of
Little, Brown Book Group
Carmelite House
50 Victoria Embankment
London EC4Y 0DZ

An Hachette UK Company
www.hachette.co.uk

www.littlebrown.co.uk

www.overcoming.co.uk

Contents

About This Book

If you have a phobia this book will explain what it is, how it keeps going and how you can go about overcoming it. To get the most from this book you must read and work through each of the parts in order from start to finish. Also, before moving on to a new part, re-reading the previous sections may help you become very familiar with them.

Overcoming a phobia requires hard work and perseverance. But the more effort you put into it, the more likely it is that you will get better, and this will make it all worthwhile. But don't feel that you have to get everything right first time. Setbacks are a normal part of the process and you can learn a lot from them.

Although this book is designed for you to use on your own, if you find that you aren't making as much progress as you'd like, ask your GP to put you in touch with a cognitive therapist who'll be able to help you to work through the process of getting over your phobia.

Brenda Hogan

Part 1: ABOUT PHOBIAS

1

What is a Phobia?

What is the difference between normal fear and a phobia? There are many situations or objects that frequently trigger fear in people. A fear becomes a phobia when it is out of proportion with the real level of danger in a situation and when it leads to reactions that are extreme. For some people, phobias can significantly interfere with their life and their happiness.

A phobia is a very powerful fear of an object or situation. This fear is extreme – out of all proportion to the amount of real danger – and is much stronger than what most other people would experience in reaction to the same thing.

What is the difference between a normal fear and phobia?	
Normal fear	Phobia
'Butterflies' in the stomach looking out the window of a skyscraper	Not accepting a job offer because it requires working in an office on the 12th floor
Feeling anxious when near a large, snarling dog	Feeling panicky and shaky when near a friendly puppy on a leash
Feeling nervous when there is a wasp nearby	Frantically running away when you see a wasp in the garden and then refusing to go back in the garden even when reassured the wasp is gone
Feeling anxious on a plane when experiencing turbulence	Not going to your best friend's wedding because you would have to fly to get there

There are many different kinds of phobias. Some phobias are quite complex – a fear of social situations is a good example. This book deals with simpler fears, known as specific phobias. A specific phobia is a fear of a particular object or situation. People with specific phobias feel very anxious if they have to face up to their fear, and usually try to escape from the situation as quickly as they can. They may also feel anxious if they think they are likely to meet the feared object or situation in the near future. Because their fear is so extreme, they will often go to great lengths to avoid the particular object or situation that frightens them.

Some people with phobias are symptom-free as long as they can avoid the feared object or situation and – for the most part – they are able to carry on with their lives normally. However, phobias and the related anxiety can become so severe that they cause problems in day-to-day living. For example, fear of needles could stop someone from going for an important medical test, and a fear of thunderstorms could prevent someone from going outside every time it looked as if it might rain.

Some common kinds of phobia

You may be surprised to learn that phobias are very common. Many people experience fear of an object or situation that is clearly out of proportion to the actual level of danger. There are many different kinds of phobia including:

- spiders
- snakes
- wasps or bees
- dogs or cats
- birds
- thunderstorms
- heights
- enclosed spaces (claustrophobia)
- blood
- needles
- tunnels
- public transport
- going in lifts
- flying in aeroplanes

Not every phobia is listed here. If yours hasn't been mentioned, don't worry. The information and strategies outlined in this book are useful tools for anyone who wishes to overcome any kind of specific phobia.

Here are two examples of people with common phobias:

Fear of spiders: Simon's story

For as long as he could remember, Simon had been afraid of spiders. He wasn't sure how or why he had developed such a fear, since he'd never been bitten by a spider and couldn't remember any specific incident that had made him afraid, although he recalled that his mother had also been fearful of spiders. He noticed that his fear seemed to get worse as he got older. Whenever he saw a spider, even a small one, he began to feel very panicky. His heart began to race, and he started sweating and trembling. At home he would shout to his wife and then quickly leave the room. He described feeling afraid that spiders were faster than he was and would certainly bite him if they had the chance. Because of his fear, Simon avoided spending time in the park with his daughter and even put off going out in the garden. He often checked corners and doorframes for cobwebs; whenever he saw one he started to feel very anxious and quickly asked his wife to sweep it away. He noticed that he even felt anxious when he saw a picture of a spider in a book he was reading to his daughter. When this happened, he quickly turned the page.

Fear of heights: Linda's story

Linda couldn't recall being afraid of heights when she was a young girl, but from her twenties onwards she developed a fear of them. She first noticed feelings of anxiety while on holiday – she began to feel quite nervous while walking along a mountain path that had a steep drop on one side. When she looked over the edge, she felt 'butterflies' in her stomach and began to feel hot and shaky. She also felt a bit dizzy, which made her worry that she might faint and fall over the edge. She quickly backed away. Returning from holiday, she began to feel anxious in several other situations, including looking out of the window of her fifth-floor office and driving over bridges. She often felt dizzy when she became anxious, which triggered worries that she might fall or lose control of her car and accidentally drive off the bridge. It wasn't long before she was avoiding looking over any window ledge above the ground floor, and would go to great lengths to avoid travelling over bridges. Eventually her fear became so severe that she even felt quite nervous when she looked down stairwells, so she started relying on lifts.

2

Where Do Phobias Come From?

'Learning' to be afraid

Some people can remember a specific incident that 'started off' their phobia, a moment when they 'learned' to be afraid. An example of this is a child who pulls a dog's tail and then gets bitten. The child is likely to be scared and distressed, may then feel afraid on seeing another dog, and may even start to avoid dogs altogether. However, what the child has 'learned' isn't entirely correct. Although it's wise to approach a strange dog with caution, not all dogs are dangerous and many are very friendly. But once the child begins to avoid contact with dogs, there's no opportunity to learn that not all dogs are dangerous. As a result, the phobia takes hold.

Not everyone who has a frightening experience develops a phobia. For example, many children are nipped or bitten by dogs and they certainly don't all develop dog phobias. There are several reasons for this. A child who's had previous experiences with friendly dogs before being bitten would be less likely to develop a phobia about dogs (although the child may still be a bit cautious around the particular dog that bit them). Or, a child who spends a lot of time around friendly dogs after being bitten would also be less likely to develop a dog phobia. In both of these cases, the child has learned that not all dogs are dangerous.

But if you can't remember a specific incident that triggered your phobia, how did the anxiety get started? You may have learned to be afraid from other people. For example, a child may have had a parent (or someone else) who taught them that dogs were scary and dangerous, and maybe even prevented the child from being around dogs. This child might grow up to be an adult with a dog phobia. Such a phobia could also develop if a child simply noticed that a parent or someone else was afraid of dogs and so believed that he or she should also be afraid. People can learn to be afraid of things even if they never have a scary encounter of their own.

Phobias that seem to come from nowhere

Many people with phobias can't remember a specific frightening incident that triggered their fear, and don't think they learned the fear from anyone else. These people may never know how their phobia started. If this is the case for you, don't be discouraged – *you don't have to know the exact cause of a phobia in order to get rid of it.*

3

What Are the Symptoms
of a Phobia?

When people come into contact with the object or
situation that terrifies them or leaves them panic-
stricken, they experience a variety of symptoms.
Physical symptoms of anxiety almost always occur.
These may include increased heart rate, sweating,
trembling, fast and shallow breathing, muscle tension
or weakness, dizziness, 'butterflies' in the stomach,
dry mouth and difficulty swallowing.

The 'fight–or–flight' response to threat

All this happens because when you feel afraid
or threatened, your body becomes 'activated' to
respond to the danger. This is known as the fight-
or-flight response, which lets your body respond
quickly and effectively to a physical threat. Our
bodies release a chemical called adrenaline that trig-
gers reactions such as:

- Your mind becomes alert and focused on the 'threat'.
- Your heart rate speeds up and your blood pressure rises.
- Blood is pumped to your muscles, which tense in order to prepare for action.
- You start to sweat more to keep your body temperature from rising too high.
- Breathing becomes rapid and shallow to provide the body with more oxygen.
- Blood-clotting ability increases, preparing for possible injury.
- Bodily processes that are not essential in an emergency, such as digestion and saliva production, slow down, causing a dry mouth, 'butterflies in the stomach' and, sometimes, nausea.

This fight-or-flight response was crucial in the distant past, when humans had to deal with physical dangers all the time. Even though we rarely face immediate physical danger in modern life, the fight-or-flight response is still very important as it helps us to respond quickly – for example, to move out of the way of an oncoming car. However, the fight-or-flight response doesn't just happen in real physical emergencies – it 'kicks in' any time we are nervous about something. And this includes situations when a physical response is not usually required. So, even if the apparent danger doesn't present a genuine physical threat, our bodies still react as though it does.

'Fleeing', 'freezing' and avoidance

Someone with a phobia confronted with the thing they fear tends to behave in one of three ways. Some people 'flee' – they leave or get out of the way as speedily as possible. Others 'freeze', feeling that they are unable to move. However, most people with phobias use avoidance – if an object or situation causes anxiety, they try to stay as far away as possible! Some people avoid only a few things, but for others, avoidance can spread to a great many objects and situations and this becomes very problematic.

Faced with a real danger or threat, it would be wise to get away from the situation and avoid similar situations in the future. Likewise, in some threatening situations, staying very still could prevent you from being noticed, which could be a life-saver. However, with phobias, these responses are not helpful. Not only are they unnecessary (remember that the fear is out of proportion to the amount of real danger), but they can also strengthen the phobia and make it harder to overcome.

Panic Attacks

The fight-or-flight response results in many physical sensations – such as increased heart rate, rapid breathing, 'butterflies' – that are uncomfortable and can be very scary. Some people react to these symptoms by getting even more anxious and may start worrying that something awful is about to happen, like they may be about to faint, go 'crazy' or even have a heart attack. These kinds of thoughts increase anxiety further, resulting in even more physical sensations, and so on – a vicious cycle of anxiety! This is called a panic attack. Panic attacks tend to last about 20–30 minutes and then slowly go away. They are not dangerous, but can be very frightening! This book contains information on strategies to help manage these kinds of anxiety symptoms. If panic attacks are a problem for you or you would like more information on panic attacks and how to manage them effectively, you can refer to *An Introduction to Coping with Panic*.

4

Why Won't the Fear Just Go Away?

Avoiding fears keeps them going

The main reason why people have trouble over-coming phobias is because they rely on avoidance as a way of managing their fear. It's natural to want to avoid something that scares you – and if this really is dangerous, then avoidance is probably a very useful strategy. But avoidance isn't very useful if your fear is out of proportion to the actual level of danger. In fact, avoidance prevents you from getting over your fear.

Remember Simon's example – he avoided going to the park or spending time in his garden because he was afraid of spiders. This tactic prevented him from learning that he was unlikely to see a spider in either of these places and that, even if he did, he was very unlikely to be bitten. It also prevented him from learning that if he went to the park and stayed there for a little while, his anxiety level would slowly diminish. Had he done these things, he would have learned valuable lessons that would have helped him get his anxiety under control.

So, while avoidance will prevent you from feeling anxious in the short term, in the long run it re-inforces the anxiety. If you always avoid the thing that scares you then it becomes very difficult for you to learn that it isn't as threatening or dangerous as you thought. It also prevents you from learning that if you faced the feared object or situation your feelings of anxiety would decrease on their own – without you having to flee.

Sometimes other people's reactions also reinforce a phobia. Friends or relatives may help the phobic person to avoid facing the feared object or situation, and so prevent him or her from learning that the situation is not as scary as they think. For instance, Simon would call his wife to sweep away cobwebs and rid the house of any spiders. Whenever she did so, it prevented him from learning that he did not need to be so afraid.

Thoughts that keep the fear going

The thoughts people have in response to the feared object or situation can also cause problems. Very often, these thoughts are about what will happen if the person faces the dreaded situation. For example, Simon was afraid that if he encountered a spider, he would be chased and possibly bitten, and Linda was worried that her anxiety might cause her to faint and fall, or to lose control of her car. These kinds of thoughts are not realistic: they simply trigger a great deal of unnecessary anxiety and can also lead to avoidance.

Not only does avoidance keep anxiety going, it can make it even worse. When you think about it, each time you avoid something, you are teaching yourself that there really is something to be afraid of. This can end up making you feel more anxious. And you may start avoiding more situations, which can then increase the anxiety even further. It becomes a vicious circle – the more anxious you are, the more you avoid, and the more you avoid, the more anxious you get!

5

What Can I Expect from This Book?

In the next section of this book you will be introduced to ways of coping with your fear. Most of these are based on the principles of Cognitive Behavioural Therapy and focus on helping you overcome avoidance in a step-by-step manner, as well as teaching you to think about your fear as rationally as possible. This has proved to be a very effective way of coping with specific phobias. Other methods, such as medication, relaxation training, counselling and hypnotherapy, are also used to help people with phobias. If you're interested in these other methods, speak to your GP to find out more.

Facing your fear – gradually!

This book mainly focuses on avoidance because this is what keeps anxiety going, and the more you avoid the thing you fear, the worse the anxiety gets. The best way to improve the situation is therefore to face your fear slowly and gradually. Exposing yourself to your fear will help you learn two very important things:

1. That the object or situation is not as scary as you first thought.

2. That your anxiety will reduce as you spend more time facing your fear.

This process can seem very frightening at first. Facing what you fear is probably the complete opposite of what you want to do! This is why you should face your fears very gradually and at your own pace. Start small.

For example, consider Linda, who was afraid of heights. She avoided travelling over bridges, looking out of windows above the ground floor, looking down stairwells, and even walking down stairs. She couldn't imagine walking near a cliff or on a mountain path! For Linda to face her fear of heights, she should start with something that causes her only mild anxiety – perhaps looking out of a first-floor window. After some practice doing this, Linda would probably find that her anxiety level came down and actually felt quite manageable. At this point, she could try something that caused her just a bit more anxiety, like opening the first-floor window and looking down. After working on this for a while, she would find that her anxiety continued to decrease. When she felt comfortable, she could move on to something a little more anxiety-provoking, like looking out of a second- or third-floor window. Once she was comfortable with this, she could practise looking down a stairwell and maybe walking down a short flight of stairs. After her anxiety levels came down to a manageable level while doing these things, she would move on to something slightly more anxiety-provoking, and so on. Slowly but surely, Linda would get closer to being able to go on a walk in the mountains. But she would never start at that step!

The next part of the book will take you through this step-by-step process in order to help you face your phobia.

Part 2: COPING WITH PHOBIAS

6

Before You Get Started

There are some things that you might want to do before you start 'facing your fear'.

Consider asking for help along the way

You don't have to have someone else's help to overcome a phobia, but it can make things a bit easier. If you decide to do this, make sure you ask someone whom you feel comfortable with and trust – perhaps your partner, a family member or a close friend. Ask the person to read this book and then spend some time explaining your fear to them. When you're ready to start trying the exercises, you may want to ask the person to accompany you and give you some support. Make sure they read about each exercise and understand what you're supposed to do. Very often, other people can be good at encouraging you to keep going and re-minding you of what you need to do to overcome your anxiety.

Learn and remember the facts about anxiety

In addition to worrying about the object of their phobia, sometimes people worry about the anxiety they will experience if they do face the thing that they fear. For example, some people worry that their anxiety might keep on getting worse or go on forever. Or they may be concerned that something awful might happen – for example, they might have a nervous breakdown, or even die. These kinds of thoughts are not helpful. Not only are they not true, they make people feel even more anxious and make avoidance more likely.

Will I faint if I get too scared? Many people are worried that the physical sensations of anxiety are a sign that they are about to faint. It is important to understand that fainting is not a side-effect of the physical symptoms of anxiety. To understand why, it is important to first explain what causes fainting.

Fainting occurs when someone experiences a sudden and extreme drop in blood pressure. However, when someone is experiencing anxiety, their blood pressure goes up, not down! This actually makes fainting incredibly unlikely.

There is one exception to this – do you, or does anyone you know, faint at the sight of blood? Or when getting an injection? This can occur with a very specific kind of phobia known as a blood-injury-injection phobia. With this kind of phobia, a person is likely to faint at the sight of blood, the anticipation of physical injury or the anticipation of an injection. It is only in these situations that the person may faint – they would not faint in other situations where they felt anxious.

This kind of fainting is not really part of a phobia at all, but rather the result of a particular biological condition. However, someone who experiences this kind of reaction may find themselves getting anxious in any situation involving blood, anticipated injury or getting or watching an injection.

So what causes it? It helps to understand that fainting is actually part of a self-protective response. Remember that fainting is caused by a sudden and significant drop in your blood pressure. Did you know that everyone has a tendency to experience a drop in blood pressure when they see blood? This is part of the self-protective response. If you see blood, there is a chance that it might be yours! And if you're bleeding, it's good to have low blood pressure, because you will bleed less.

However, a small proportion of people have an extraordinarily strong response to seeing blood (or injuries, or seeing/having an injection) – their blood pressure drops more than average, and enough to make it difficult to get adequate blood flow to the brain. If your blood pressure drops significantly, the part of your body in the most trouble is your brain, because it's at the top. The brain needs a steady and constant supply of blood, and it can be damaged if blood flow is impaired. Fainting is the body's response to this problem. If we can't get enough blood to the brain, fainting creates a situation where the brain is brought down to the blood (because it results in a change of posture from sitting or standing to lying down). This is part of the self-protective process.

So how can this be dealt with? Fortunately, there is treatment for this problem, but it is a bit different from how other specific phobias are treated. Many of the same strategies discussed in this book are used, but add-itional techniques are taught to reduce the chance of fainting. To stop the fainting, the person learns how to raise their blood pres-sure, usually by tensing and squeezing large muscle groups (like the thighs) while they are in their feared situation (this can be prac-tised while looking at medical photographs, syringes, or while having an injection). If the person can keep their blood pressure up, they will not faint. Note that tensing the muscles is the opposite of relaxation, which is what would likely be helpful if you had any other kind of phobia.

You can certainly use this information to work on a blood-injury-injection phobia on your own. However, if you feel like you need more support due to the unique nature of this kind of phobia, it can be helpful to talk to your GP and/or work with a cognitive therapist to help overcome the problem.

So what are the facts about anxiety?

1. Anxiety can make your body feel very un-comfortable and it's not uncommon for people to worry that it might cause serious physical or mental problems. This isn't true. Anxiety is a perfectly normal physical reaction – it's not dangerous and doesn't cause nervous breakdowns.

2. Anxiety won't keep rising endlessly and doesn't go on forever – it may go up, but it always comes back down again.

3. The first time you try something that frightens you, you're likely to feel anxious. However, if you stay in the situation long enough, your anxiety levels will come down, as you begin to realise that the situation isn't as dangerous as you'd thought. Furthermore, the physical symptoms can't go on forever. The 'fight-or-flight' response (see pages 12–14) is a short-term physical reaction, and your body is designed to 'calm itself down' after a little while.

4. If you keep practising the exercises, you'll begin to notice that you feel less anxious and that the anxiety starts to come down more quickly. The more you practise, the better it gets!

Prepare coping statements

It can be very helpful to use coping statements when you are working to overcome your phobia. Remember that anxiety is fuelled by negative, anxiety–provoking thoughts. These thoughts may be as simple as 'Oh no!' when you see a feared object or enter a feared situation, but they can also be thoughts such as 'I can't handle this!' or 'I've got to get out of here!' These kinds of thoughts serve to increase anxiety and increase the likelihood that you are going to try to escape or avoid the feared object or situation, thus serving to keep the anxiety going. Coping statements are positive statements you can purposely make to yourself just before or while you face your fear that will help you decrease your anxiety and decrease the likelihood that you are going to run for the hills.

It is very helpful to prepare these statements in advance. Spend some time writing these thoughts down in a notebook. You may even want to write them on cards or on your phone, so that you can keep them with you and look at them when you need to (when your anxiety is high these thoughts may be hard to remember!).

Below are some examples of coping statements you could use before or during an exposure exercise. These are just examples – try to think of other coping statements that are specific to you and your situation. Try to address the negative or anxiety-provoking thoughts that bother you the most. You may also find it helpful to include some of the facts about anxiety (see previous pages).

Examples of Coping Statements for Preparing to Face your Fear

- Each time I face my fear, it is a step closer to getting rid of this phobia

- Each time I face my fear, it will get a little bit easier

- I can do this!

- I will feel better once I'm in the situation – the anticipation is the worst part

- Nothing bad is going to happen

- My anxiety is not dangerous – I am going to be fine

- I may feel anxious, but I can handle this. The physical sensations of anxiety are normal and not dangerous. I am not going crazy!

Examples of Coping Statements During a
Phobia Exposure

- I can handle this

- Relax, breathe slowly

- Nothing bad is going to happen. I'm
  going to be all right

- I can do this!

- I'm doing this

- This is easier than last time

- The feelings will pass

- It's just adrenaline making me feel this
  way

- I'm anxious, but I'm OK! I can keep
  functioning

Spend some time learning how to relax

Remember the physical symptoms of panic attacks?
These symptoms (e.g. racing heart and sweating)
can be anxiety-provoking in themselves! It's a good
idea to practise some techniques to help you relax
and reduce these physical symptoms.

One very useful technique that can be used to ease the physical symptoms of anxiety is controlled breathing. When very anxious, people often 'over-breathe' – this means that their breathing becomes shallower and faster. Sometimes over-breathing is very obvious, but at other times people don't realise that their breathing has changed. Breathing more quickly and shallowly is not dangerous – it is the same way you breathe when you exercise. But if you breathe like that when you are not exercising, there are some uncomfortable side-effects, such as light-headedness, dizziness, feeling 'faint', tingling sensations and even vision changes. Strangely, one side-effect of over-breathing is that it can make you feel as if you are not getting enough air. This can lead to the mistake of trying to breathe more. In fact, trying to breathe more or gasping for extra breath will make the symptoms worse, not better. Again, this isn't dangerous, but it will result in temporary discomfort.

You can learn to correct over-breathing by using controlled breathing. This means focusing on breathing gently and evenly through your nose, filling your lungs completely and then breathing out slowly and fully. Controlled breathing may sound easy, but it actually takes practice. Using controlled breathing effectively can help reduce the physical symptoms of anxiety.

Controlled breathing

At first, it may be easier to do this exercise lying down, or sitting in a comfortable chair. As you become more experienced with controlled breathing, you can try the exercise sitting upright or standing.

1. Place one hand high up on your chest and one lower down on your stomach.

2. Breathe in slowly through your nose, allowing your stomach and chest to swell gently. Look down at your hands. Is your lower hand moving? Good. This means that you're using all your lung space, not just panting from the top of your lungs. Ideally, you should see gentle movement in both hands. If you can't see any movement, try to push your stomach out very slightly as you breathe in – this will encourage breathing using the whole of your lungs.

3. The in-breath should be slow and gentle and quiet – other people should not be able to hear you breathe.

4. Pause briefly.

5. Breathe out slowly and gently.

6. After breathing out, pause for a moment. Don't take the next breath in until you feel it is 'time'. (This does not mean 'holding' your breath – just a slight pause.)

7. Repeat this process. Try to get a rhythm going. Keep the breathing slow and deep and gentle.

Learning to relax your muscles is also useful. When you're under stress, the muscles in your body become tight and tense. Learning how to relax in response to tension can help you reduce physical tension, become calmer, and lower your overall level of anxiety. Like controlled breathing, relaxation is a technique that takes practice.

Opposite, you will find a set of instructions for progressive muscle relaxation. This exercise teaches you how to identify muscle tension and then to go from a state of tension to a state of relaxation. It works by getting you to tense the muscles in a part of your body for about 5 seconds, and then relax them for 20 seconds. This process helps you to recognise when your muscles are tense and teaches you how to release that tension and give way to relaxation.

The first few times you try this you'll probably need to rely on the instructions. However, with a bit of practice, you should be able to work through the exercise on your own. When you feel ready, you can reduce the amount of time you spend prac-tising and use your skills whenever you feel you need them. Eventually, you will become better at noticing when your muscles are tense, and will be able to relax them 'on-the-spot', without having to tense them first. This is a helpful technique to use when you feel yourself getting nervous.

Progressive muscle relaxation

1. Lie down and start by taking a couple of deep breaths. Focus on your breath-ing, and let your muscles slowly relax. Breathe slowly and gently. Feel yourself beginning to relax.

2. Turn all your attention to your feet. Tighten the muscles by raising your feet and pointing your toes towards the ceiling. Hold this position for about 5 seconds. Then relax the muscles. Con-centrate on the changes in sensation in your muscles as they move from a tense state to a relaxed one. Focus on the feel-ing of relaxation for about 20 seconds.

3. Now tighten the muscles in your hips and legs by pressing down on your heels. You should feel tension in your calves and in your upper legs. Hold this position for about 5 seconds, and then let go. Relax. Focus on the feeling of relaxation for about 20 seconds.

4. Move your focus to your abdomen. Tighten your tummy muscles as much as you can. Focus on the tension for about 5 seconds. Then let your abdomen relax. Keep your attention on the feeling of relaxation for about 20 seconds.

5. The next step concentrates on your chest muscles. Take a deep breath. Hold it. Feel the tension around your rib cage. Then breathe out, and feel the changes in your chest as you do so. Breathe in deeply, fill your lungs, hold it, notice the tension, and then breathe out. Let your chest muscles relax. Return to slow and gentle breathing.

6. Progress to your hands and forearms. Place your hands palm up. Squeeze them into fists, and turn the fists towards the ceiling. Focus on the tension

(about 5 seconds), and then let go. Let your hands and arms relax. Focus on the relaxed feeling for about 20 seconds.

7. Now for your upper arms. Create the tension by pressing your hands down as hard as you can. Hold it for 5 seconds, then let it go. Focus on the relaxation in your arms (about 20 seconds).

8. And now, your neck. Tense the muscles in your neck. Hold the tension for about 5 seconds, and then relax. Focus on relaxing your neck muscles for about 20 seconds.

9. Your shoulders are next. Shrug your shoulders to tense the muscles. Pull your shoulders up towards your ears. Hold the position (5 seconds). Then slowly relax. Let your shoulders gently drop back down. Focus on the feeling of relaxation (about 20 seconds).

10. Now your mouth and jaw. Clench your teeth and pull your mouth into a forced smile. Your mouth and jaw should feel very tense and tight. Hold it (5 seconds) and then relax your face. Focus on the feeling of relaxation for about 20 seconds.

11. Move up to your eyes and nose. Close your eyes as tightly as you can, and wrinkle your nose. Hold for 5 seconds. And then relax. Focus on the relaxation for about 20 seconds.

12. Finishing with your forehead, raise your eyebrows as high as you can. Hold the position for 5 seconds, focusing on the tension and tightness. Then relax. Focus on relaxing (20 seconds).

13. You have now gone through all the muscles of your body. Continue to relax, and each time you breathe out, allow yourself to become even more relaxed. Each time you breathe out, think of a part of your body, and then allow the muscles to relax even more.

14. When you've completed the exercise, take a moment to let yourself become more alert. Open your eyes, and move your arms and legs around a little bit before you get up and start being active again.

7

Identifying Your Fear and Setting Goals

Before you go any further, you need to think about your fear. What is it that frightens you? Try to be as specific as possible – for example, it might be only big spiders or black dogs that cause you anxiety. It's also important to think about what you're afraid might happen if you face your fear. For example, Simon was afraid that he might be bitten or chased by a spider, and Linda was afraid she might faint and fall, or lose control of her car. Write down your fear below:

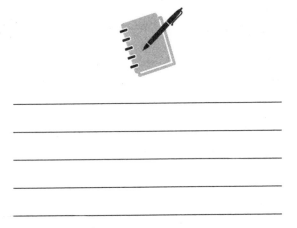

_____

_____

_____

_____

_____

It's useful to think about what you'd like to achieve by overcoming your phobia. Is there something specific that you'd really like to be able to do that you've avoided, or had trouble with, because of your fear? Think about what your phobia has prevented you from doing. Then set yourself a goal you can work towards.

Your goal will depend very much on your circumstances and what's important to you. It doesn't have to be extreme – you may not have any desire to be able to handle a tarantula if you have a spider phobia, or to go out climbing cliffs if you have a height phobia! That's fine. Your goal should reflect what you personally want to achieve. And your goal should be manageable. For example, for someone who was fearful of flying in aeroplanes, it probably wouldn't be feasible to be ready for a transatlantic flight in a week's time.

Think back to Simon and Linda. What kind of goals might they set? Simon, who had a spider phobia, might set the goal: 'I want to be able to stay calm when I see a spider in the house – be able to put it in a cup and take it outdoors.' Linda, who was afraid of heights, might set several goals: 'I'd like to be able to cope with (1) looking out of a fifth-floor window, (2) driving over bridges, and (3) walking down any set of stairs.'

What is your goal? Write it down below:

_____

_____

_____

_____

_____

_____

8

Learning to Rate Your Fear

You've probably noticed that your level of fear varies quite a bit. In some situations you feel only mild anxiety, while in others you feel very scared. As you work through the exercises in this book, you'll be asked to rate your fear. This will help you judge just how anxious you feel in different situations, and will also help you measure any reductions in anxiety that you experience.

Fear can range from nothing (i.e. you feel safe and calm) to the worst anxiety imaginable (i.e. you're completely terrified). When you are asked to rate your fear, give it a number on a 0 to 10 scale, in which 0 represents no fear at all and 10 represents the worst anxiety imaginable.

0	1	2	3	4	5	6	7	8	9	10

$\longleftarrow \qquad\qquad\qquad\qquad\qquad\qquad \longrightarrow$

| no fear | | mild fear | | moderate fear | | | severe fear | | | worst fear |

Whenever you are asked to rate your fear, you can imagine marking an X somewhere on this line between 0 and 10.

9

Creating a List of Feared Situations

For most people, the level of fear tends to vary in different situations. For example, someone with a phobia about thunderstorms might find driving a car during a thunderstorm causes more anxiety than looking out of the window at a storm. And both of those situations might produce more anxiety than watching a film of a thunderstorm.

Using a notebook, piece of paper or a computer or smartphone, create a list of situations that cause you different levels of anxiety, including some that cause you only a mild amount of anxiety, some that produce moderate levels of anxiety, and others that make you extremely anxious. This will help you decide where to start. Remember, the plan is for you to begin by exposing yourself to situations that cause you lower levels of anxiety, and gradually work up to situations that provoke higher levels of anxiety.

Begin by considering all the different situations that cause you anxiety – think about the situations, tasks or activities that you have been avoiding. Make a list of these. For each item on your list, put down a fear rating from 0 to 10. Then put your list in order, starting with the situations that don't cause you much fear at all, and building up to the situations that you find the most frightening (and therefore avoid the most). The point of this exercise is to work out a list that reflects the full range of situations that you fear and avoid.

Here's Simon's list as an example:

Looking at a cartoon picture of a spider	0
Looking at a photograph of a spider	1
Playing with a plastic spider	2
Walking through the garden	3
Looking under furniture or in corners for spiders	4
Looking at a small spider in a jar	5
Looking at a large spider in a jar	6

Watching a spider crawl across the table	7
Watching a spider crawl on someone else's hand	8
Catching a spider in a glass	9
Spider crawling on own hand	10

When creating your own list, make sure you include a wide range of situations that make you anxious – from situations that are only mildly anxiety-provoking, through situations that are a bit scarier, to situations that cause a very high level of anxiety. The more situations, the better – try to come up with more than ten if you can. Give each a rating between 0 and 10, and then put them in order from lowest to highest.

• Think of as many different situations as you can. Use more than one page if necessary.

• Take your time making your list. Give it lots of thought. You may need a few days to think it over and come up with enough situations to cover the whole range of fear.

• You can always add more situations to your list later on, and you can change the order if you think you got it wrong the first time.

Troubleshooting: What if I'm having trouble making my list of feared situations?

If you have some trouble compiling a full range of situations covering the whole gamut of anxiety, try asking yourself these questions:

- What if someone was with me? Would this reduce my fear rating?
- What if I was alone? Would this increase my fear rating?
- What if I tried this in an unfamiliar setting?
- What if I imagined my feared object or situation? How would this affect my fear rating?
- What if I watched a film that involved my feared object or situation? How anxiety-provoking would that be?
- Does how close or far away I am from the feared object make a difference?
- If I watched somebody else doing what I fear, how anxious would I be?

Your answers to these questions may help you think of some new situations that will fill in any gaps in your list.

10

Facing Your Fear

It is now time for you to start facing some of the situations that you find difficult.

Review your list. Select one of the situations that you rated as only mildly scary (for example, something you rated between 1 and 3 out of 10). This is the situation that you'll work with first.

There are two very important rules to follow:

1. When you are facing a scary situation, stick with it as long as you can! Remember your anxiety level will decrease the longer you stay in the scary situation. It may be helpful to decide what your goal is in advance – for example, you will try to stay in the scary situation until your fear rating comes down to a 1 or a 2.

2. Repeat each exposure until you feel comfortable. If you can, repeat it several times in a row. You will also want to repeat it over several days. The goal is to get to a point where the situation is not causing your anxiety to rise above

a 3. As you work through your list to the more highly fear-rated situations, you may find that you need more exposure time in order to start feeling comfortable.

Remember that you are almost certainly going to feel uncomfortable. It is very normal to feel anxious and to experience physical symptoms of anxiety (such as pounding heart, 'butterflies', and sweating – see page 15) when you are facing a scary situation. You should expect to feel this way! It is important to remember that these feelings will gradually decrease the more times you face your fear.

Getting support – from others and from your own rational thinking

Sometimes it can feel a bit scary to get started. If you are feeling nervous, there are a couple of things you might want to try.

First of all, this is a good time to ask for help from a close friend or family member. Having someone there to support you can make things easier. You can try facing the situation alone later on, when you feel more confident. Also, it's sometimes easier to start by watching somebody else doing what scares you – then you can try it yourself.

Tips for your support person. It is a great idea to have your support person read this book before you get started. Here are a few pointers to help them understand what they can do (and not do!) to support you in this process:

Do

- Provide reassurance

- Use distraction (talk, point out other things in the environment)

- Provide encouragement (to persist until the anxiety comes down)

- Provide reminders to use breathing or re-laxation strategies and coping statements

- Give praise for efforts and successes (even if small!)

- If possible, go into the situation first – watching someone else cope in the situation (especially if you are a bit anxious yourself!) can be helpful

- Let the person with the phobia go into the situation on their own when they are ready

Don't:

- Push too hard – the person with the phobia gets to decide when to leave the situation

- Criticise, judge, or say things like 'try harder!'

Second, try to think about what you are about to do as rationally as you can. Your coping statements can help you with this! It is easy for your thoughts to spin out of control when you are anxious, and your positive coping statements can help you stay calm(er) and keep you focused. Remember the facts about anxiety (see pages 30–1) – you may even want to include these in your coping statements. Try to make your coping statements as meaningful to you as you can. For example, it was helpful for Linda to remember that anxiety would not cause her to faint, so it was very unlikely that she would fall down and hurt herself, or that she would lose control of her car. Sometimes, people have other thoughts about their feared situations that they know are a bit unrealistic or 'out of proportion'. For example, Simon rationally understood that the vast majority of spiders were not dangerous and it was very unlikely that a spider would chase him (although he often worried about it anyway!). So it helped Simon to remind himself that walking through the garden was safe, and even if he did see a spider it would not chase him.

Here are a few other examples:

Irrational Thought	Rational, More Helpful Thought
That lift is going to break down – I will be trapped and will suffocate.	It is highly unlikely that the lift will break down. I cannot remember ever hearing of someone suffocating in a lift. There are air vents in lifts.
The plane will crash.	I do not know anyone who has ever been in a plane crash. Plane crashes are very rare. Turbulence happens all the time on aeroplanes – it does not mean the plane will crash.

Think about any irrational or exaggerated thoughts you have about what might happen when you face your feared object or situation. Then think about what would be more realistic to say to yourself as you face your fear. Write down your more realistic thought as a coping statement in a notebook. Keep adding to your list of coping statements as you work on facing your phobia. You may find that some coping statements are more powerful than others, so the more you have to choose from the better! Remember to use these coping statements before and while you face the situations that scare you.

Using practice records

It's important to fill out a practice record as you try out the situations on your list. A practice record will enable you to keep track of: what you do, how anxious you thought you would feel, how anxious you really were, and what the outcome was.

Here's a practice record for Linda, who was afraid of heights:

Date: 1 January

Target situation	Expected anxiety	Actual anxiety	Outcome
Looking out of a first-floor window	3	2	Anxiety dropped after a few minutes – felt a bit dizzy but it went away – didn't faint
30 minutes later – looked out of the window again	3	1	Anxiety dropped further
The next day – looked out of a first-floor window	2	1	Anxiety dropped after a few minutes – didn't get dizzy
30 minutes later – looked out of the window again	1	0	Anxiety disappeared almost immediately

Use the blank record overleaf to make your own
practice record for your first exposure exercise. Downloadable versions are available on the
Overcoming website, but you can also create your
own in a notebook or on a computer. Start by com-
pleting the first two columns – write down what
you are planning to do, and then rate the level of
anxiety you expect to experience. Then go ahead
and do it!

Date:

Target situation	Expected anxiety	Actual anxiety	Outcome

When you have finished, rate the level of anxiety you actually experienced and write down the outcome of the event. For example, you may have noticed that your anxiety levels came down. Or you may have noticed that what you feared did not occur! Whatever happened, write it down.

Remember to do your exercises several times, until you consistently feel that your anxiety is manageable in the situation. You'll probably need to repeat each exercise many times over the course of several days – just keep doing it until you feel comfortable.

It's important to make and complete a practice record each time you try to face a new feared situation.

Remember

- Start small
- Stick with it as long as you can
- Repeat the exposure until you feel comfortable
- Repeat the exposure over several different days

Reviewing your progress

After you've completed a few practice records, review your progress. Look at what you have written in the 'Outcome' column.

- Did your anxiety levels come down? If so, remember this as you face more difficult situations. Most people find it comforting to remind themselves that the longer they stay in a situation, the better they will feel.

- Did what you fear most really happen? If not, remember this as you work up to the more challenging situations on your list. For example, Linda was relieved to discover that her anxiety came down quite quickly during her first few practice exposures (and she did not faint!). She reminded herself of this as she tried more difficult exposures. Simon discovered that, far from wanting to bite him, most spiders seemed to be afraid of him and quickly scurried away. Once he became a little bit more convinced that the spiders he encountered in his house and garden were not dangerous, it was easier for him to move on to the more difficult exposures, like catching a spider in a glass.

- But supposing what you feared did happen? The important thing is that you faced it. And if you managed to cope, that's particularly important.

Sometimes it's very helpful if the 'worst' happens – because it teaches you that you can handle things even when they go wrong! For example, when Simon first looked under furniture for spiders, he saw one crawling straight towards him! At first, he felt very panicky and quickly moved away, but then he managed to go back and stay still until the spider moved away on its own. Although this experience was very scary for Simon, he learned that he could cope when he became very frightened and that the spider wasn't dangerous.

What if you feel you are taking two steps forward and one step back? Setbacks are normal! One day you may feel like you made great progress and the next day your anxiety seems worse. This is typical. This is one of the reasons that keeping a practice record is so helpful – it will help you see that you are making progress overall, even though it may be harder to see day-to-day.

11

Facing More Difficult Situations

Once you feel comfortable facing the first situation on your list and you've repeated the exposure exercise on several different days, you're ready to move on to the next item. This situation should provoke a bit more anxiety than the one you've already dealt with.

Remember that it's important not to 'escape' by leaving the situation. Stay in it as long as you can. This will help you prove to yourself that nothing awful is going to happen, and that your anxiety levels will come down despite being in the presence of the thing you fear. Repeat the exposure until you feel comfortable. When you feel you've mastered this situation, it's time to move on to the next item on your list. Each time you challenge yourself by facing your fear, complete a practice record (see page 58).

As you move down your list, you may find that you need to stay in the scarier situations longer before your fear dies down. You may also need to do more exposures over more days. This is fine – just keep at it until your anxiety feels manageable. You can never do too many exposure exercises!

Troubleshooting:

What should I do if my anxiety level feels too high or doesn't seem to be coming down?

- It's important to give yourself enough time to let your anxiety come down. This can take a while. A few minutes may not be enough for anxiety levels to come down to a manageable level. Some people find that they need 30 to 45 minutes before they feel comfortable, and for others it takes even longer.

- Think as realistically as you can. Remember the facts about anxiety (see page 30) and remind yourself about the real level of danger in a situation. It's helpful to review the outcomes from your previous exposures.

- If you find it helps, use controlled breathing (see pages 35–6) or progressive muscle relaxation (see pages 37/40) during the exposure to make you feel calmer.

- One of the keys to getting over a phobia is to repeat your exposure to it. Once in a while is not enough – you are much more likely to notice an improvement if you practise every day.

- Have you moved down your list of feared situations a bit too quickly? Try going back to a situation on your list that is less scary and do that again until you feel comfortable. Don't move on to the next step until your anxiety has come down to a manageable level. This can take a little while, so be patient. Remember to stay in the feared situation as long as you can, and use re-laxation techniques if you need to.

- Another possibility is that there may be too much of a 'jump' between items on your list. It can be quite difficult to move from a situation that provokes a small amount of anxiety to a situation that provokes quite a lot of anxiety. If you think you might be taking too big a step, try to think of some other situations that cause 'in-between' levels of anxiety to help bridge the gap. These situations should provoke less anxiety than the situation you are having trouble with, but more anxiety than the last situation that you managed successfully. Work through these situations before you return to the one that was causing you problems.

• If you have requested the help of a friend or family member, you can always ask them to do the task first so that you can watch. This can be a good way of preparing for a challenging exposure. Even when you are watching someone else, you should complete the practice record.

• Another good way of preparing for a challenging exposure is to imagine it first. Again, complete the practice record – imagining a scary situation is also an exposure.

• If you find that none of these strategies work, then it may be helpful to keep working on the particular exposure that is causing you problems. Stay in the situation as long as you can, but if you start to feel overwhelmed, allow yourself to temporarily retreat from the situation. Use controlled breathing, relaxation and coping statements to help bring your anxiety down to a lower level. Then, return to the feared situation, and repeat the same process. If you can stay longer than the first time, that's great, but if you don't, that's okay too. Repeat the process multiple times and repeat it again over multiple days, and be sure to complete your practice record so you can see your progress. For the situations that are the most difficult, it may take some time and repeated effort to bring the anxiety down to a manageable level.

It may take a while, but you should be able to make your way slowly through the feared situations on your list. If you find that things are getting too difficult, look back at the previous parts of this book. You may need to work on each step longer as the situations get more challenging. Most people find that it takes several weeks of regular practice before they're ready to tackle the situations they find the most anxiety-provoking. Don't worry if it seems to be taking a while – do it at your own pace.

The stories below should give you some more ideas about how to face up to your own feared situations.

Sheryl's story

Sheryl's fear of birds seemed to have started when she was a teenager, but she couldn't recall a specific frightening incident involving a bird. Her phobia had become worse as she got older. Sheryl was most afraid of pigeons and doves. Smaller birds, such as sparrows, and larger birds, such as ducks and geese, were less frightening for her. She wasn't sure why this was so. She found it difficult to explain what exactly was so frightening about birds. But she said she was quite worried that a bird might fly at her head, or perhaps peck or claw her. She avoided places where there were large numbers of birds, like parks and public areas in her village. She decided to set herself the goal of being able to walk slowly and calmly through a busy public area where there were lots of pigeons and doves.

Sheryl's list of feared situations looked like this:

Feared situation	Fear rating
Looking at photographs of birds	1
Watching birds from a window (while inside)	2
Walking through a park where there are a few birds around	3
Sitting in a garden or park and watching birds from a distance	4
Going to a pet shop, zoo or aviary and looking at birds in cages	5
Going for a walk beside a local river and watching ducks and geese (getting within 2 to 3 metres of the birds)	6

Feeding ducks and geese at the river's edge	7
Going to a park or public area where there are lots of pigeons and doves and watching the birds from a distance	8
Slowly getting closer to pigeons and doves in a public area	9
Freely and calmly walking through an area with a large number of pigeons and doves	10

Sheryl slowly began working through her list, beginning with the situations that provoked the lowest levels of anxiety and gradually working up to the more frightening ones. She wrote down what happened after each exposure. This helped her to realise that birds were in fact very unlikely to fly at her head or peck or claw her. As she began putting herself in situations that provoked higher levels of anxiety, like feeding ducks and geese, she found it helpful to remind herself that the birds were not dangerous. With her husband's encouragement, she was able to try scaring the birds. This showed her that, when she made sudden movements, the birds were likely to fly away from her, rather than towards her. Sheryl tried to remember all this whenever she tried a new exposure. She repeated each exposure many times until she felt comfortable. It took about six weeks of regular practice, but Sheryl was eventually able to walk or sit near birds, including pigeons and doves, with only very slight levels of anxiety.

Brian's story

Brian was phobic about thunderstorms. He couldn't recall feeling afraid during thunderstorms as a child, but as an adult his phobia had become quite severe. He was terrified that, whatever building he happened to be in, he was at great risk of being struck by lightning during a storm. During a thunderstorm, he felt panic-stricken. If he was at home, he'd shut himself in a cupboard (so that there were no windows through which he might see lightning). He'd also play music loudly through earphones so that he'd be unable to hear any thunder. If he wasn't at home, he'd lock himself in the toilet and close his eyes. Although thunderstorms were quite rare where he lived, he carefully monitored the weather reports many times each day, and checked the Internet and newspapers for long-range weather forecasts. He felt quite nervous if it was grey and cloudy, and sometimes would even avoid leaving the house (or wherever he happened to be) if it was raining outside. This avoidance behaviour caused him problems, as it sometimes interfered with him getting to work and meant that he often cancelled social plans. Brian's goal was to be able to stay out of the cupboard when there was a thunderstorm, and to be able to function normally if the weather was overcast or rainy.

Brian's list of feared situations looked like this:

Feared situation	Fear rating
Looking at photographs of lightning and storms	1
Listening to an audio recording of a thunderstorm when it's sunny outside	2
Not being able to check the long-range weather forecasts	2
Watching a video or film that includes footage of a thunderstorm	3

Listening to an audio recording of a thunderstorm while it's raining outside	4
Not being able to listen to many daily weather reports	4
Going for a 30-minute walk when it's overcast	5
Going for a 15-minute walk when it's raining	5
Going for a 30-minute walk when it's raining	6
Going to work or to a social event even if it's raining or overcast and there's a possibility of a thunderstorm	7
During a thunderstorm – not using the earphones but still going into the cupboard	7
During a thunderstorm – using the earphones but not going into the cupboard	7

During a thunderstorm – not going into the cupboard or using the earphones but watching television instead	8
During a thunderstorm – looking out of the window	9
Walking from a building to the car during a thunderstorm	10

It took Brian many months to get over his phobia about thunderstorms. This was because thunderstorms were really quite rare where he lived, so it was difficult for him to practise managing his most feared situations. He had to wait until thunderstorms happened – but when it took months for a storm to occur, he realised that thunderstorms were not as frequent as he had thought. This made it easier for him to do some of the things that he found moderately anxiety-provoking, like going outside when it was overcast or raining. After each practice situation, Brian wrote down what happened, which helped him remember that what he feared (a thunderstorm in which he or the building he was in was struck by lightning) didn't actually happen.

Brian found that he had to repeat many of the situations on his list over and over again. For example, it took him quite a while to feel comfortable listening to and watching audio and video clips of thunderstorms, particularly when it was raining outside. Because thunderstorms happened so infrequently, he often tried to imagine thunderstorms. He would close his eyes and imagine a storm while he was listening to an audio recording of heavy rain and thunder. This made him feel quite anxious at first, but after a while he felt much better. He said that imagining thunderstorms helped prepare him for the 'real thing'.

A year after starting to work on his phobia, Brian said that he felt able to manage his anxiety during a thunderstorm. He was able to walk outside when it was raining and had completely stopped checking the weather forecast. He wasn't entirely free of anxiety during a thunderstorm, but he was able to stay out of the cupboard.

Elsie's story

Elsie had claustrophobia (a phobia about enclosed spaces). She remembered this being a problem even when she was very young – she used to refuse to play games like hide-and-seek with her friends because she dreaded the thought of hiding in a small, dark place. As an adult, her claustrophobia began to affect her life a lot more. She avoided using lifts (even though her office was on the sixth floor) and public transport. She avoided using public toilets. When she was at home, she didn't close her bedroom door at night and would use the toilet upstairs and not have to close the door. She felt nervous at work when she went to meetings and the door was closed, although she managed to tolerate this. Elsie wasn't quite sure why she was so nervous in enclosed spaces. However, she did know that she worried that she would be unable to get out, which might lead to her panicking and making a fool of herself. Elsie set quite a difficult goal for herself – she wanted to use the lift at work every day, even though she hadn't been in a lift for over ten years!

Elsie's list of feared situations is shown on the following pages.

Elsie used several different strategies to help her work through her list. She reread the facts about anxiety (see page 30) before each practice exposure, and repeatedly reminded herself that her anxiety wasn't dangerous and would decrease the longer she stayed in the enclosed space. She wrote down what happened each time she practised an exposure. When she read over the outcomes of the exposures she had done, she was able to see that (go to page 78):

Feared situation	Fear rating
Sitting in a large room with windows with the door shut (30 minutes)	1
Sitting in a small room with windows with the door shut (30 minutes)	2
Going to bed with the door only a few inches ajar	3
Sitting in the upstairs toilet with the door only a few inches ajar	3
Sitting in a small room with the curtains drawn and the door closed	4
Going to bed with the door closed	4
Sitting in the upstairs toilet with the door closed	4

Sitting in the upstairs toilet with the door closed and locked	5
Sitting in the downstairs toilet with the door closed	5
Sitting in the downstairs toilet with the door closed and locked	6
Going into a public toilet that is not busy and closing the cubicle door	6
Going into a public toilet that is not busy and locking the cubicle door	7
Going into a busy public toilet and locking the cubicle door	7
Travelling a short distance (10 to 15 minutes) on a bus or train	8
Travelling a long distance (over 1 hour) on a bus or train	9
Using an empty lift	9
Using a lift with other people present	10
Travelling on a plane	10

1. Her anxiety levels usually came back to normal levels after about 20 or 30 minutes.

2. Even when she felt very anxious she didn't lose control and was able to sit still.

3. Each time she repeated an exposure it got easier. She found this very encouraging.

Elsie did find that she got 'stuck' when she reached the more challenging items on her list of feared situations. Although she was able to use public toilets comfortably, she felt very nervous about using public transport or lifts. At this point, she decided to ask a friend to help her. The first few times she took a bus, her friend travelled with her and reminded her to think rationally and to breathe slowly and gently. Elsie said that she was able to relax when she realised that she wasn't suddenly going to 'lose control' and ask the driver to stop the moving bus to let her off. She also asked her friend to accompany her on a short train ride. When this went well, Elsie was able to take a train ride by herself. She said she felt very anxious at first, but as usual, her anxiety slowly decreased.

Elsie then began using lifts. Again, she asked her friend to help her. She made sure the lift was empty by going into the office at the weekend. At first, she only travelled up one floor, but she slowly worked up to six floors. Then she practised doing it by herself, without the help of her friend.

When she finally managed to take the lift on a workday with other people present, she was very nervous, but she was so pleased with herself she was convinced she could do it again.

The next day, the worst happened. The lift stopped between floors. Elsie panicked: she felt hot and sweaty and she started to cry. But she also said that other people in the lift were nervous too – one person started banging on the door and another shouted for help. Someone else put his arm around her shoulders to comfort her. The lift only stopped for a few minutes before it began moving again and she was able to get out. She said she felt quite shaken after this experience, but she was surprised and relieved that she hadn't been the only person who was anxious, and that no one had laughed or stared when she started to cry. In fact, one person was quite sympathetic and tried to comfort her. After a few days, she decided that she would tackle the lift again. A month later, she was very proud to report that she had taken the lift every day and was feeling much more confident. She was even thinking about going on a holiday abroad, which meant that she would have to go on a plane.

12

Reaching Your Goal and Staying on Top of Things

Remember the goal you set? Have you reached it yet? If so, congratulations! If you haven't yet reached your goal, you may want to plan how you will work towards achieving it. If you're already feeling less anxious, this may be fairly straightforward. But if you do still feel anxious about your goal, make a plan. Write out the steps you'll have to take to reach your goal, and work on them gradually, one by one. Remember: start small, stay in each feared situation as long as you can, and repeat each step until you feel comfortable. Think about your fear and your planned exposures as rationally as you can. Ask a friend or family member to help you if you need it.

Rewarding yourself

Once you've reached your goal, reward yourself! There are lots of different ways you could do this.

You might decide to go out for a special meal or a day trip, or perhaps buy yourself a new item of clothing or a nice bottle of wine. You don't have to spend extra money – another reward could be to allow yourself the opportunity to do something enjoyable, like spending some time on a favourite hobby, going for a walk with your partner, or preparing a special meal at home. You deserve it – you have worked hard.

You should be very pleased with yourself if you've managed to face your fear and are now feeling less anxious and more able to do the things that you want. You'll want to make sure that you don't let that fear creep back in – and if it does, you'll want to be able to get it back under control again.

Keeping the fear away

How can you prevent the fear from coming back? The most important thing is to keep facing the object or situation that has given you so much trouble in the past. If you start avoiding it again, then you may very well find that the fear comes back. The more you face the feared object or situation, the less anxious you will feel.

This may mean going out of your way to put yourself in contact with the feared object or situation.

For example, if you're dealing with claustrophobia, make sure you take the lift once in a while, even if it's quicker to take the stairs. If you're afraid of heights, go out of your way to look out of windows and down stairwells. If you're afraid of spiders, you might decide that you will get rid of every spider that is found in the house, rather than asking your partner to do it. If you continue to face the object or situation you used to fear, you will make it very difficult for the fear to come back.

What if the fear does come back? This may happen if you start to use avoidance again, or if you don't manage to keep yourself in regular contact with the feared object or situation. This does not mean that you are back to square one – this time, you know what to do! Just follow the steps outlined in this book. And keep this book handy, so you can refer to it whenever necessary.

Other Things that Might Help

This book has provided you with an introduction to the problems caused by phobias and what you can do to overcome them. Some people will find that this is all they need to do to see a big improvement while others may feel that they need a bit more information and help, and in that case there are some longer and more detailed self-help books around. Using self-help books, particularly those based on CBT, has been found to be particularly effective in the treatment of anxiety-related problems. Ask your GP if there's a Books on Prescription scheme running in your area – if there isn't, we recommend the following books:

Mastery of Your Specific Phobia (Treatments That Work) by Michelle G. Craske, Martin M. Antony and David H. Barlow, published by Oxford University Press

Overcoming Anxiety by Helen Kennerley, published by Robinson

Phobias and How to Overcome Them: Understanding and Beating Your Fears by James Gardner and Arthur H. Bell, published by New Page Books

Sometimes the self-help approach works better if you have someone supporting you. Ask your GP if there's anyone at the surgery who would be able to work through your self-help book with you. Some surgeries have Graduate Mental Health Workers who would be able to help in this way, or who might offer general support. He or she is likely to be able to spend more time with you than your GP and may be able to offer follow-up appointments.

For some people a self-help approach may not be enough. If this is the case for you, don't despair – there are other kinds of help available.

Talk to your GP – make an appointment to talk through the different treatment options on offer to you. Your GP can refer you to an NHS therapist for Cognitive Behavioural Therapy – most places now have CBT available on the NHS, although there can be a considerable waiting list. Don't be put off if you've not found working through a CBT-based self-help manual right for you – talking to a therapist can make a big difference. If an NHS therapist isn't available in your area or you'd prefer not to wait to see one, ask your GP to recommend a private therapist.

Although CBT is widely recommended for anxiety-related problems there are many other kinds of therapy available that you could also discuss with your GP.

Medication can be very helpful for some people and sometimes a combination of medication and psychological therapy can work wonders. However, you need to discuss this form of treatment and any possible side-effects with your doctor to work out whether it's right for you.

The following organisations offer help and advice on phobias and you may find them a useful source of information:

Triumph Over Phobia
Tel: 0845 600 9601
Email: info@triumphoverphobia.org.uk
Website: www.triumphoverphobia.com

British Association for Behavioural and
Cognitive Psychotherapies (BABCP)
Tel: 0161 705 4304
Email: babcp@babcp.com
Website: www.babcp.org.uk

Provides contact details for therapists in your area, both NHS and private.

An Introduction to Coping with Health Anxiety

2nd Edition

Brenda Hogan and Charles Young

ISBN: 978–1–47213–851–4 (paperback)

ISBN: 978–1–47213–952–8 (ebook)

Price: ₺4.99

This book offers guidance for those whose health anxiety or hypochondria have become serious problems and are having a negative impact on their mental health. Through the use of cognitive behavioural therapy (CBT), expert authors Brenda Hogan and Charles Young explain what health anxiety is and how it makes you feel, showing you how to spot and challenge thoughts that make you anxious and reduce your focus on illness. Written in a concise and accessible way, this book gives you both an understanding and an aid for combatting this often-neglected psychological problem.

An Introduction to Coping with Insomnia and Sleep Problems

2nd Edition

Colin Espie

ISBN: 978-1-47213-854-5 (paperback)

ISBN: 978-1-47213-892-7 (ebook)

Price: £4.99

Poor sleep can have a huge impact on our health and wellbeing, leaving us feeling run-down, exhausted and stressed out. Written by a leading expert in the field, this simple guide explains the causes of insomnia and why it is so difficult to break bad habits. It gives you clinically proven cognitive behavioural therapy (CBT) techniques for improving the quality of your sleep, showing you how to keep a sleep diary, set personal goals, improve your sleep hygiene, deal with a racing mind and make lasting improvements to your sleeping and waking pattern.